Stopping By Woods On A Snowy Evening And Other Plays

Nine monologue plays
by Don Nigro

A Samuel French Acting Edition

FOUNDED 1830

SAMUELFRENCH.COM
SAMUELFRENCH-LONDON.CO.UK

Copyright © 2012, 2015 by Don Nigro
All Rights Reserved
Cover Art by Anna S. Contessa

STOPPING BY WOODS ON A SNOWY EVENING AND OTHER PLAYS is fully protected under the copyright laws of the United States of America, the British Commonwealth, including Canada, and all other countries of the Copyright Union. All rights, including professional and amateur stage productions, recitation, lecturing, public reading, motion picture, radio broadcasting, television and the rights of translation into foreign languages are strictly reserved.

ISBN 978-0-573-79989-1

www.SamuelFrench.com
www.SamuelFrench-London.co.uk

For Production Enquiries

United States and Canada
Info@SamuelFrench.com
1-866-598-8449

United Kingdom and Europe
Plays@SamuelFrench-London.co.uk
020-7255-4302

Each title is subject to availability from Samuel French, depending upon country of performance. Please be aware that *STOPPING BY WOODS ON A SNOWY EVENING AND OTHER PLAYS* may not be licensed by Samuel French in your territory. Professional and amateur producers should contact the nearest Samuel French office or licensing partner to verify availability.

CAUTION: Professional and amateur producers are hereby warned that *STOPPING BY WOODS ON A SNOWY EVENING AND OTHER PLAYS* is subject to a licensing fee. Publication of this play(s) does not imply availability for performance. Both amateurs and professionals considering a production are strongly advised to apply to Samuel French before starting rehearsals, advertising, or booking a theatre. A licensing fee must be paid whether the title(s) is presented for charity or gain and whether or not admission is charged. Professional/Stock licensing fees are quoted upon application to Samuel French.

No one shall make any changes in this title(s) for the purpose of production. No part of this book may be reproduced, stored in a retrieval system, or transmitted in any form, by any means, now known or yet to be invented, including mechanical, electronic, photocopying, recording, videotaping, or otherwise, without the prior written permission of the publisher. No one shall upload this title(s), or part of this title(s), to any social media websites.

For all enquiries regarding motion picture, television, and other media rights, please contact Samuel French.

MUSIC USE NOTE

Licensees are solely responsible for obtaining formal written permission from copyright owners to use copyrighted music in the performance of this play and are strongly cautioned to do so. If no such permission is obtained by the licensee, then the licensee must use only original music that the licensee owns and controls. Licensees are solely responsible and liable for all music clearances and shall indemnify the copyright owners of the play(s) and their licensing agent, Samuel French, against any costs, expenses, losses and liabilities arising from the use of music by licensees. Please contact the appropriate music licensing authority in your territory for the rights to any incidental music.

IMPORTANT BILLING AND CREDIT REQUIREMENTS

If you have obtained performance rights to this title, please refer to your licensing agreement for important billing and credit requirements.

CONTENTS

Stopping By Woods On A Snowy Evening......................5

Gringonneur......................11

Lagoon......................21

Mermaid......................29

Just Out The Corner Of Her Eye......................37

Portal......................43

Listening......................51

Nothingness......................59

Muse......................67

Stopping By Woods On A Snowy Evening

For Anna Contessa

*It is easy to love
the Kaleidoscope Girl
and you'll be very happy
you met her.*

*It is easy to lose
the Kaleidoscope Girl
but impossible to
forget her.*

*Nobody knows
how many people
she has been.*

CHARACTER & SETTING

There is one character, **JASMINE**, a woman of 28, who speaks from a circle of light on an otherwise dark stage.

(**JASMINE**, *a young woman, speaks from a circle of light on an otherwise dark stage.*)

JASMINE.
I like being looked at,
but it's also horrible.
I know. That doesn't
make any sense.
But most of the things I feel
don't make any sense.
Everything is half a contradiction.
Every explanation is a lie.
Every declaration of love
is a betrayal.
I live in this place
and people look at me
and they all think
I'm beautiful
and they all want me
and some of them are nice
and some of them are the
lowest form of human sewage
and I've been looked at so much
and desired so much
and told I was loved so much
that I can't tell them apart now.
I don't know who to trust
and who not to trust
so sometimes I trust everybody
and then I don't trust anybody
and everything gets
so strange and sad and lonely

because there's too many people
jabbering at me and
looking at me
and wanting me
and wanting to touch me
and sometimes I
think I just can't
deal with this any more.
I just can't.

Who do these people think I am?
Because I don't know.
They think I'm somebody else.
They love somebody else.
I want them to look at me
and then I just want them
to go away. I want everything
to just go away.

And when I feel like that,
there's this place
in my head, where I go
sometimes to hide.
Whenever things get to be
too much. And I feel like
there's such a fire in my brain
that I'll never be able to
think clearly or be calm again.
It's this place near where we lived
when I was a little girl.
By the woods.
I would go there when I was
sad or unhappy and
I could feel myself just
calming down.
And in the winter

in the early dark
with the snow falling
you could actually hear
the snow falling
and I'd think of my
favorite poem, the one
about stopping by woods
on a snowy evening,
and in the midst of my
loneliness and my sorrow
I'd feel this unspeakable,
unearthly joy welling up
in me. It was the woods
and the snow and the poem
and something that would
resonate in my soul.

But lately
when I reach for that place
in my head,
I can't find it.
It's like I've forgotten
how to get there.
It's like a dream where
you need to be someplace,
like somebody you love
very much is going to be
at that place, and
you need to get there
before they go away forever.
But somehow you make a
wrong turn, and end up in
this other place, and you're
lost, and you can't get back
to where you were going

and this other place, this place
you're lost in, it's oddly
familiar, as if you've
been there before,
like you could open any
door in any other place
and you'd find yourself
in this lost place, these
empty streets, this
desolate place.

That's what I'm looking for now.
I keep looking for the door
in my head that when I open it
that snowy woods will be there.
And everything will be so still
you can hear the snow falling.

(The light fades on her and goes out.)

GRINGONNEUR

CHARACTER & SETTING

There is one character, **GRINGONNEUR**, a painter, who speaks to us from his studio in Paris.

TIME

The year is 1392.

AUTHOR'S NOTE

In the year 1392 King Charles VI of France ordered the painter Charles Gringonneur to create for him a new deck of Tarot cards. This was also the year in which the King of France went mad..

(Sound of dogs yapping and barking, howling at the moon. **GRINGONNEUR** *in a circle of light, speaking to us from his studio.)*

GRINGONNEUR.

Gringonneur, said the King. I want you to design a pack of cards.

Of late it has now and then been His Majesty's affectation to speak to me as if he were cast in a puppet play as my brother. He cocks his head to one side and grins crookedly at me when he speaks, squinting as if the sun were in his eyes. He has affected this uneasy, false camaraderie since the Queen sat for her portrait with me. He always seems to be politely refraining from mentioning that he could have me drawn and quartered at any time.

The trouble with the cards began when the King got separated from his drunken companions while out hunting in deep woods, and stumbled upon a camp of gypsies. As he was drinking from the wineskin a man with a scar on his mouth offered him, his royal gaze happened to fall upon a girl who was gently shuffling a worn pack of Italian playing cards. The girl was attractive, and the King had an eye for that sort of thing, but to his surprise he found his attention being drawn to the greasy cards she was laying out on a wooden table.

The pictures on these cards seemed to him at once odd and enigmatic, and yet somehow familiar, almost as if he'd painted them himself, in another life. The dogs howling at the moon. The man with ten swords in his back. The naked lovers. The girl bound and blindfolded.

He asked the gypsy girl to tell his fortune. She shrugged, shuffled the cards, and offered him the deck to cut. When he placed his hand upon the cards, they seemed to burn the flesh of his palm. The girl laid out the cards, and stared at them.

Well? said the King. What is my fortune? Will I make love to a beautiful gypsy?

She looked for a moment longer, then scooped them up and tied them in a scarf.

What is it? What's the matter? said the King. What did the cards say?

The cards don't speak, said the girl. And if you ever hear them jabbering at you, you mustn't listen to them.

When the King realized the girl really had no intention of telling him what the cards said, he became angry, and threatened to have them all killed, but the gypsies just stared at him, and since he was alone, surrounded by them, and completely at their mercy, he thought it prudent to get back on his horse, from which superior position he reached down on impulse and ripped the scarf with the cards out of the girl's hands and rode off, which he felt perfectly justified in doing, since it has always been the duty of kings to steal from the poor.

Somehow he found his way back to the hunting party, and tried to lead them to the gypsy camp, to teach the romanies a lesson about respect for authority, but the gypsies were nowhere to be found.

So they rode back to the palace, where that night, and for many nights after, the King spent hours arranging the cards in different combinations, staring at them, trying without success to reproduce the exact configuration the gypsy girl had laid out for him.

But the gypsy's pack is filthy, said the King, and the figures drawn rather crudely. I want the same titles and pictures, just done in a less vulgar manner. Copy them, but copy them better. In a way that is not so disturbing.

In fact, the King seemed not completely himself. Nervous. Feverish. He tossed me a knotted up scarf with something inside. For a moment I fancied that it moved, just slightly, as if some living creature were trapped in there. Here are the cards, he said. When you have made me a clean version, destroy these.

And then he looked sideways at me so oddly, so furtively, that I became convinced there was something about the cards he wasn't telling me. But what could I say? I couldn't refuse the King. So I thanked him for the honor, and took the little bundle home with me.

When I was alone in my studio, I undid the knotted scarf, and a greasy pack of cards dropped out upon the table like a toad. They were filthy objects, creased and worn at the edges. The pictures were faded and slightly smeared. And yet the crude figures on the cards were absolutely spellbinding.

A Fool, a Magician of some sort, a Hermit holding a lantern, the Devil, Death. The images were oddly powerful, and, as with the King before me, gave me the eerie sense that I had somehow known them in a previous life.

And now, as I work, painting the King's new deck, the faces on the cards begin to inhabit my dreams. I can't get them out of my head. The Hanged Man. The naked girl who is the World. And I feel that, in some way I can't explain, I'm making things that are alive. Or they are making me.

A message from the Queen: the King's gone mad. Has he caught the madness from these cards? Will I catch it next? And someone's rearranging my furniture at night. And I hear whispering from other rooms.

Sometimes, in my troubled dreams, I am the King, lying in my bed at night with the sleeping Queen, my hand resting on her naked back, terrified that the cards will crawl out of the knotted scarf, climb up the bedclothes and begin eating the flesh off my face. I have long suspected that what a person makes devours him. Our creations devour us. Our children devour us.

I am the servant of what I create. Painting the cards has become everything to me. I love the smell of the paint. I love the colors. The colors are sex. To create is to absorb the madness that surrounds you. Experience is like the plague. You catch the thoughts, the passions, hatred, pain, of everything you paint. One is possessed by a demon who makes things using your eyes and fingers. The cards are impossibly ancient. How can something I myself have created be so much older than I am? The cards are alive. Wait. Calm down. Listen. This is how it happens:

The King goes to Brittany to punish the Duke for plotting to murder him. The army is riding slowly through a dark forest labyrinth, then suddenly emerges onto a vast plain. The sun is very bright in their eyes, after the gloom of the forest. Then, as if from nowhere, a ragged, wild eyed man appears, running towards the King, seizes the bridle of his horse, shouting Turn back. One of us is betrayed. The soldiers are about to kill the lunatic, but the King forbids it. He's not sure why. The madman looks familiar to him somehow, as if he's seen him once, long ago, in a mirror. So the ragged man follows them for miles, screaming and wailing, until the King, blinded by the sun shimmering off the armor of his knights, very hot, and filled with increasing terror, hears the loud clang of a lance dropped by a sleepy page strike the side of a helmet, and begins attacking all the horsemen around him in a frenzy. It takes ten men to subdue the King.

The expedition returns home. The King lies dazed, stammering nonsense, recognizing no one. Gradually, he seems to improve. Then one night, at a drunken masquerade to celebrate the King's return to his senses, a group of courtiers, dressed as wild animals, coated with pitch and shreds of hemp and tied together for some purpose which is unclear, somehow come into contact with a torch and catch fire. Most of the wild men burn to death. The King survives only because the Duchess du Berry throws her gown over him, squats and urinates on him. Fortunately, she has drunk a great deal of punch.

But the King's relapses come more and more frequently. Doctors and other charlatans are consulted in great numbers, sorcerers suspected of casting a spell on him are questioned and imprisoned. In the midst of his babbling, the King speaks repeatedly of a pack of cards.

But it does not matter if the King is a lunatic. It does not matter that I shall very likely never be properly reimbursed for the time and effort I spend making these cards. When the King, even a mad King, commands, one obeys. So I continue to work, deeply immersed in the world of the cards. Time loses all meaning for me. I hear snippets of gossip from the palace. The King has declared his son a bastard and the Queen a whore. The King speaks gibberish he believes is ancient Babylonian. The King orders suicidal cavalry charges. The King holds long conversations with puppets.

In my dreams I see puppets looking round corners at me. What is that noise? Who is whispering downstairs in the dark at night? Is this real? There are times when I wonder if I am real. Could I be dreaming now, when I think I'm awake? Or could I be part of the King's dream? Everything in my experience now seems to have some sort of occult significance. Because everything is a symbol, whether you want it to be or not, whether you understand what it is a symbol of or not. The cup. The staff. The knife. The naked girl at the end of the world. The symbol gives rise to explosions of meaning, geometrical progressions, dimension within dimension, like mirrors reflecting mirrors. Terrifying. With cherries. Did the King give me these cards to drive me mad? Did he suspect that I was the Queen's secret lover? Was this his revenge for fathering his wall-eyed, lopsided heir?

God is urbane and monstrous. Sleeping, belching, farting, hiccuping into a greasy napkin. God's crooked fingers and bloodshot eyes. His infernal cackling. I want to break God's nose with a broom handle. There is something in these cards, some principle of order which is in fact a diagram of the lunacy inside God's brain. Listen, listen, listen. What?

I will tell you a secret. I can see the Devil in a small piece of blue glass which I keep for that purpose. The wind blows through the house, opening and closing doors at its own discretion. I am caked and splotched with paints, mostly purples and reds. I talk to myself as I work, mumbling, swearing, laughing under my breath. I have rheumatism of the elbows, but I don't care. The floor of my studio is made of great squares like a chess board. The madness of a monarch is a reflecting mirror. It reveals backwards the madness of God. And as the King is God's representative on earth, and his madness God's madness, this is God's revenge. I look in the piece of blue glass and see myself lying dead in my studio, my throat cut by one of the cards. The King is a glass puppet.

They are alive. The cards are alive. The symbols in the cards are alive. They are a distillation of many thousands of years of suffering and humiliation. Here in this forest of symbols, I hang myself upside down. I am the Juggler, the Crooked Magician, the Beggar. They jabber at me constantly. I can almost make out what they're saying. No. Shut up. Shut up. Quiet. Quiet.

A gypsy girl comes to model naked for me. I am hypnotized by her breasts. Or is that the Queen? Is one being driven mad by paint fumes? Does the painter believe he is the Mad King? Or does the Mad King believe he is the painter? Fool. King. Painter. We are all members of the same mad company.

A scent of new mown hay. A fragment of broken mirror. A red, blotchy face in the mirror like a rutabaga. The house is full of cats and smells of fried liver and onions. Caked and splotched with paints. Mumbling, swearing, laughing under his breath. Rheumatism of the elbows. A woman's elbows.

Sometimes I'm fine for months. Then lightning strikes the ruined tower and my head is on fire again. Sometimes I can't remember my name, don't know that I am King, believe that I am a painter named Gringonneur who sleeps with the Queen. I don't know my wife. Who is this woman? I wish she would leave me alone. I don't know my children. I run wildly through the palace. They have walled up the entrances. They have turned it into a labyrinth. I am lost here. I won't change my clothes. I refuse to bathe. I am made of glass. I am terrified that I will break.

The English are invading. My bastard son wants to kill me. They are whispering to me, always whispering. The gypsies have come in the night to steal back the soiled deck of cards. Perhaps the soiling is part of its power. Shuffle the deck. What difference does it make how we order information? That which is random is infinite. In chaos is encompassed all possible meanings. Seventy-eight versions of the King's Madness. Each one contains a naked girl. I have seen her in a blue glass which I keep for this purpose. I kiss the Queen's breasts.

I juggle, do some tricks, sell spells and charms of various sorts, play and sing a bit, perform skits with a small company of puppets. I am the gypsy with the scar on his mouth. I am the King who stole the cards. I am the painter he ordered to paint him new cards. I am the juggler who posed for the cards with the naked girl. I am all the people on the cards. Shuffle the deck. The ultimate act of love is to willingly share the madness of another. Allow me to read your fortune. I see unfathomable darkness.

(The light fades on him and goes out.)

Lagoon

CHARACTER & SETTING

There is one character, Meredith Cherry age 18, who speaks to us from a circle of light surrounded by darkness.

TIME

Meredith lives in Armitage, a small town in east Ohio, in the autumn of the year 1954. It's night.

*(**MEREDITH**, a girl of 18, speaks to us from a circle of light on an other wise dark stage. It's a rainy night in the autumn of 1954 in Armitage, a small town in east Ohio.)*

MEREDITH.

The Creature from the Black Lagoon is always in my dreams. But lately, not just there. He's here. He's in town. How he got all the way from his secret Lagoon in the Brazilian rain forest to a small town in east Ohio, I don't know. He must have migrated from one body of water to another, and ended up in Grim Lake, which is probably the only place around here he could hide in for long. Then at night he crawls out of the lake and sneaks across town, hiding in the bushes, to get to my house. He must really love me, to have left his Lagoon and come all this way. Or else he really wants to eat me. Like Captain Hook's crocodile. We're all descended from cannibals.

Storm tonight. The wind rattles the windows and the doors. In the darkest part of the night, ticking clocks, dogs barking, something knocks over a trash can in the alley. Rain beating against the windows, gurgling in the gutters. Lying on my back in bed, staring into the patterns forming and reforming on the ceiling in the dark, something in the house.

Sometimes I hear him downstairs at night, fumbling around in the kitchen, rattling pots and pans. I don't know what the hell he's doing down there. Making a ham sandwich? One morning I found a cucumber on the floor. What did he want with a cucumber? Should I go down there and get him some hot chocolate?

But then he started coming upstairs. You can tell when the Creature is coming because of the smell. He smells like a swamp. But to be fair to him, it's not an entirely unpleasant smell. It smells a little like sex. I don't know if he can smell himself or not, since he doesn't have a nose. He's got a mouth like a frog and no nose but he's still kind of attractive, in a way. He looks like he works out.

I lie in bed at night, pretending to be asleep, and I hear the door creak, and these squishy footsteps on the carpet, and he comes over to the bed, and he leans over me, breathing on me. I'm confused about that. He's got gills. So if you've got gills, why do you breathe through your mouth? I feel the creature above me, and I don't move, and I don't open my eyes. I'm shaking so bad, but I don't open my eyes. In the morning there are still wet spots on the carpet, and in the bed, and bits of water grass.

I think about him all the time. Peeling an orange. Peeing. In the bath. Maybe he's lonely. I think most monsters are lonely.

I've always been drawn to monsters. Frankenstein's monster, of course. I'm really obsessed with that whole complex thing. The Green Man that lives in the woods and is made of mud and leaves and God knows what. I used to walk up on the Ghost Hill and feel him there. I think the Creature from the Black Lagoon is maybe the water-based version of that guy. Bogles, my Grandma Bessie used to call them. This girl is always seeing bogles, she said. She's got the gift. But every gift is a curse.

When I was a little girl I thought I saw the Devil looking in the window at me. And even before the Creature showed himself, I had a very strong sense of the presence of something. If I'd light candles, something would blow them out. If I looked in the mirror, I'd think I could see, just for a moment, a glimpse of something just over my shoulder.

The first time I saw the Creature was at the Drive In Movie, from the back seat of Jim Rainey's Chevy, but I was kind of busy at the time, with Jim's hands on my breasts. Up under my dress. His fingers in my panties, probing. And up on the screen, the Creature corners the pretty girl with the long bare legs. Him on top of me. Shoes off, breasts bare, skirt up. My toes clutching onto the seat covers. I remember thinking my bare feet looked like some other girl's feet. His hand between my legs. Something goes into the Sibyl's cave. Something else comes out. Penetration. Violation. To have the monstrous thing inside you.

I wonder how many women the Creature has had, and how did he know about me? It must be some sort of telepathy. I draw him with my thoughts. Maybe when I was watching the movie at the Drive In he could feel my brain waves. Does he murder all the women he loves?

But the unexpected thing about the Creature is, so far he's been a gentleman. Why does he hesitate to ravish me? Does he not have a penis? He's part fish. Does a fish have a penis? I really wish I'd paid more attention in biology class. Or does he sense, somehow, that there's life growing inside me, and does that put him off his game? He likes my hair. He always smells my hair.

At first he terrified me, but now when he doesn't come, I miss him. Some nights I go downstairs and walk around the house, looking for him. In the dark, empty study at night, the lingering smell of my father's pipe. My father sits in front of the fire, reading Shakespeare. He misses my mother desperately, still, although it's been years since she abandoned us. Love is a terrible thing.

Something always itching at the inside of my head.

I climb down the rose trellis and go for long walks alone in the dark, and I can hear the Creature following me. He makes little squishing sounds when he walks.

Sound of trains in the night. Something scuttling in the tool shed in back. My life is a tangled ball of yarn. Walking alone by the cemetery. Sometimes the darkness is the best defense. I dream of trains and bloody clothing. Deep in his Lagoon, what does the Creature dream?

There is a stranger inside me. Keep calm, Ophelia. My father read it to me. There is a willow grows aslant a brook. I hope all will be well. We must be patient. There's rosemary. That's for remembrance. Rue's for repentance.

I don't feel like eating, but the thing inside me is hungry. Devouring me. It lives in the lagoon inside me. Wolves eat the moon. Tormented. The Devil's face at the window. I can smell the Creature in the house.

I lay out the tarot cards again and again, looking for a future in which I'm not crazy or dead. I got them at Esau Van Vogt's curiosity shop. He gave them to me. Take them, pretty girl, he said. They're old and dirty but there's power in them. No charge for a pretty girl like you. They say he stuffed his wife and keeps her in the upstairs parlor. The Hanged Man. The Ruined Tower. The naked girl who is The World. The question is what to do. Fear death by water.

Fallen trees in the woods. The drifting of leaves in the water of Pendragon Creek. A white snake with blue eyes on the pile of bricks, the ruined kiln by the brickyard.

The monster sees the girl swimming. He falls in love. He takes her to his hidden cave in the Lagoon. I am falling into a miasma.

I helped Mrs McCaffrey with Sherry's birthday party. A circle of little girls in the basement, in chiffon dresses, doing the hokey pokey. Ben's sad face at the top of the steps. Poor little boy. Already, the despair of love. Did he see us, that night I was babysitting, when Jim came over? I'd put him to bed. There was a Bela Lugosi movie on the little Philco television. Late at night, in the dark, just the ghost light of the television set, Jim Rainey on top of me on the sofa. Was Ben watching from the doorway? Did I hear him disappear up the stairs? It must have looked to him like some monster was attacking me. Put the key in the lock, and turn the knob.

I dream of trains shrieking in the night, and bloody clothing on the tracks.

There's another world, just at the edge of ours. Sometimes you can sense it, almost feel it there. But when you reach out touch it, it's gone.

Playing rummy with my father. Playing chess with him. My father reading Shakespeare by the fire. How my mother hurt him. Rue's for repentance. How can I tell him? I want to but I can't. He'll be so disappointed in me. My mother made my father's life a living hell. And now I do, too. And I will make it worse when I tell him. No. I can't tell him.

Making love among the ferns on the Ghost Hill, the last time I saw him, when I told Jim about the baby. Smell of burning leaves. He said not to worry. He said he'd think about it.

They found him on the railroad tracks by the brickyard in the morning. He had a duffle bag with him full of clothes. He was leaving town. But somehow, a passing train got him, cut in him into pieces. There's still a big splattering of dried blood there on the tracks. They said he'd been drinking. But I know what happened. It was the Creature. The Creature pushed him onto the tracks.

The Creature is the voice in my head. He is my own personal monster. Come out to the lake, says the voice in my head. Come into the water. Just walk out into the water. And the water will close over your head. And everything will be cool and dark. Those are pearls that were her eyes.

And I tell myself that I must resist this voice. Because of the stranger inside me. But out my window, I can hear the mourning of the Creature. I can feel his longing, his terrible sadness. He longs for me to join him. He wants to pull me under. And then I'd never have to tell my father.

No. I mustn't do that. I mustn't.

And yet, it must be very cool at the bottom of the Lagoon. Very peaceful there, in the dark water. Where my beloved monster waits for me.

(The light fades on her and goes out.)

Mermaid

CHARACTER, SETTING, & TIME

There is one character, **INSPECTOR JOHN RUFFING**, an old man. The year is 1940. The place is the south coast of England, somewhere near Rye. Night.

(Sound of gulls. Lights up on **RUFFING**, *a well preserved old man, a retired police inspector, by the ocean, somewhere on the coast of England, near Rye, in the autumn of the year 1940.)*

RUFFING.

I've never liked the ocean much. I don't trust it. Never learned to swim. But now they've sent me here, an old man in time of war, to make these foolish solitary foot patrols, looking for submarines, saboteurs, smugglers, ghosts, I don't know. I walk the shore each night. But all I can think of is her.

She was always drawn to the sea. She was terrified of the water, but she loved it. She loved what terrified her. Not just the water. All sorts of danger. Dangerous places. Dangerous situations. Dangerous people. The fear seemed to excite her. The mysterious. The violent. The dark.

Why, then, did she love me? Was it because she thought she saw the darkness in me? Perhaps, in the beginning, she feared me. She was perhaps under the impression that I was a rather dangerous fellow. She had mistaken me entirely, which is not uncommon in matters of sexual selection. I had a dangerous profession, of course, but that is not the same thing at all, which, as soon as she came to realize—

Did you hear that? Is that a light? Is something out there? No. The moon, moving across the water.

She grew up on the coast, near Land's End, and she and her sisters would sneak out of the house at night and swim naked in the ocean. What was forbidden was what attracted them. Three beautiful young girls. They were like three sirens, calling me onto the rocks.

And there was another there with them, an older boy, a controlling, violent, superficially charming boy—charming to her, at least. Although from the first time I heard his voice, he made my flesh crawl.

And this boy would bait her into swimming out too far into the ocean. Much farther than was safe, towards the mythical land of Lyonesse, which legend said now lay deep beneath the waters. She was terrified and excited, and that feeling remained in her.

When we were first married, she would take me out to the shore at night, take off her clothes, and run into the water, like a savage. Impossible behavior. But I couldn't stop her. I never could deny her anything she wanted. Except I wouldn't go in the water with her. I'd stand knee deep in the waves calling to her. She always swam out too far. She swam like a mermaid. It seemed to remind her of some dark place in her mind she feared but was somehow being drawn back to.

She was always restless. She would get up in the middle of the night and walk through the house, out into the back garden. I never knew what she was looking for. Her inexorable attraction to that which could destroy her was balanced, for the first few years of our marriage, with her intense love for me, and for our child, but there was something that kept gnawing at the inside of her head, something that could not let her rest. She heard voices. But she never would tell me whose voice, or what the voices said.

When she was depressed or in a kind of nervous distracted frenzy I would do my best to comfort her. I talked to her, sometimes for hours, telling her stories, reciting fragments of old poetry, anything to distract her. And she would talk to me about her childhood, stories about lost girls and mermaids and such that seemed to mean something to her I could not quite fully grasp. I listened. I held her. I think the only times in my life when I have ever been truly happy were when

I was holding her, and she was, for a time, comforted. But other times, and increasingly as time went on, when she was depressed or upset, she would move instinctively away from me, away from comfort, not towards it. As if somehow I, who loved her, and would have died for her, was the enemy, and that which would destroy her, somehow, her friend.

She was a kind of dancer on the edge of oblivion. I wanted so desperately to save her from falling, from drowning. But of course I could not. Those are pearls that were her eyes.

Her eyes. Her eyes would change color. And sometimes she would look at me as if the person inside her were being taken over by somebody else. I could look into her eyes and see her trapped inside, terrified, as if she were being possessed by some demon.

She's been gone for so long.

Time has always mystified me. I do not understand time. I am not religious. I am not superstitious. I have no beliefs. I know that she is lost to me forever and yet it feels to me sometimes as if she is just on the other side of a thin, transparent wall. I keep wanting to reach through that wall to get to her. To touch her again. Sometimes the telephone rings, in the middle of the night. I pick it up, and there's no one there. And I know it's her. I just know it's her. But where is she calling from?

My father repaired clocks, kept clocks, had a shop full of ticking clocks. A little bell above the door would ring, when somebody entered. All the clocks said different times. They would chime all night at odd hours. And sometimes at night I would go down to the shop, from my upstairs room, and sit in the dark in the ocean of ticking clocks. It was like being inside God's brain. And nights when she would disappear from the house, I would sit in the dark and wait for her, amid a sea of ticking clocks.

There is a painting of a mermaid on the shore. Her back is turned. We see her naked back as she turns to look towards a child. I have a memory of her in this pose, on the bed, her naked back turned towards me. She has turned away from me, but her naked back, curved like the mermaid, is so beautiful. I reach out to touch her. Then I wake up. I do not think that they will sing to me.

But I have, of late, walking upon this shore at night, been almost certain that I heard something. Something like music, singing, I fancy, out there, in the water. I know it's just the sound of the waves crashing against the rocks, or of sea birds, the ringing of distant bells, but it seems to me—and I have dreamed of this—it seems to me that she is calling to me. From out there in the water.

Foolish, of course. The mind finally goes. After years of desperate over use, of trying to solve riddles with no solution—after years—I close my eyes and what I see is her naked back, kneeling on the bed, turning away from me, but in doing so deliberately giving me this gift, this vision. Characteristic of her that in the moment of most intense connection and tenderness between us she would turn away from me to give me this gift, what I see now each time I close my eyes.

It is a lie that mermaids have no tears.

Why are you crying? I said.
Because I am a character in a play, she said.
Because I am half girl and half something else.
Because I dream about terrible things which
happened to me when I was somebody else—

Her eyes. To look into the soul of another and see one's own death.

To love is to willingly share another's madness.

We grow by a process of organic accretion. We decline in a sort of mirror image of this process. In each stage we long to be in the other.

Memory is a sort of palimpsest. A manuscript or piece of writing on which the original writing has been effaced to make room for later writing but of which traces remain.

A pile of clothing, left on the shore, but no sign of her. She drowned, they said. Slipped out of the house one night, took off her clothes, went into the water, and never came back. A verdict of drowning, possibly intentional.

I do not believe she drowned herself. I do not believe that she would deliberately abandon her child. Or me. I do not believe that. But I also do not believe it was an accident.

At night I dream that birds fly out of the mirrors.

The mermaids decorate their gardens with the bones of former lovers. A labyrinth of bones. Clutching in their fingers the bleached bones of men. And oft in the long still nights of June we sit on the rocks and watch the moon. We sit on the rocks.

Once we lay in the moonlight, looking at the lights of the town, in the distance. I could feel her heart beating against me. No one comes here but the dead.

A little bell above the door of the shop would ring. A sea of ticking clocks.

The garden has become a tangled wilderness. My mind has become a labyrinth of darkened passageways. We sit on the rocks and watch the moon.

At night I lie in the dark and I can hear her voice in my head. She beckons me to come to the ocean. She beckons me into the water. I stand here looking out each night.

She calls to me.

Walk into the water, she says.

If you love me, walk into the water.

Do you hear that? There is something out there. There's somebody out there.

Perhaps if I just walk out a little ways.

(The light fades on him and goes out.)

Just Out The Corner Of Her Eye

For Anna Contessa

CHARACTERS

There is one character, **JASMINE**, a woman of 28, who speaks from a circle of light on an otherwise dark stage.

(JASMINE, a woman of 28, speaks from a circle of light on an otherwise dark stage.)

JASMINE.

I run away a lot. Sometimes I just can't help it. I think I'm doing all right, and then suddenly I feel this overwhelming urge to be someplace else. It's a kind of panic, I guess. Something in my head. Things get too close, I get scared, I run. It feels as if—it feels as if something is closing in on me. As if something's been watching me, listening to me, waiting for a chance. And I can sense it, just before it's about to get me. And I run. I don't want to run. I can't help it.

I understand that this is an illusion. It's probably an illusion. There's probably nothing after me. But when your life's at stake, how sure can you afford to be? Besides, that's a lie. I know there's something. It's because of the patterns.

I see patterns. I've always seen them. But lately, more and more. In carpets. In nature. In my life. Evidence of design. And not just of design. Of a kind of malignant watchfulness on the part of somebody or something. Signs. There are signs everywhere, if you just look. Most people don't want to look. They don't want to know. But I can't help it. The world is a forest of symbols, and I can see them. It's like everything's written in some sort of code. But I don't have the code book. Or maybe like I had it once and lost it.

I suppose this is how superstitions and religions start. Somebody thinks they see a pattern. It could be an illusion. Or it could mean something. You can't be sure. But there's a part of you that actually wants to believe there's a pattern, even if you don't know what it is. But you want to know what it is.

Or, let's say there is no pattern. Let's say everything is random. If everything is actually random, then all the patterns we think we see might as well be illusions. But that can't be. Because the patterns are there. And some of them clearly mean something. It's not just like the constellations, where you look at a group of stars and decide it's a bear or a spoon or something, even though you could draw different lines through the stars and see an entirely different pattern, and in fact the stars that look like they have some relationship to each other are actually at impossibly vast distances away from each other. They only look like they're close together because of the accident of where we're looking at them from. If we were looking at them from a different place, there'd be totally different patterns. But some patterns are not the result of an arbitrary figure/ground configuration. Some patterns have significance. Blood splatter, for instance. If you look at blood splatter, you can use the patterns to reconstruct events in the past. You look at the splatter of blood and you can tell that somebody did something terrible to somebody in a certain way with a certain weapon from a certain angle. So understanding patterns can be a kind of time travel evidence that the whole idea of the past is not some sort of illusion.

So where do the patterns come from? Well, suppose God constructed the universe as a kind of puzzle for us to solve. And he's left these clues. But he's made it so difficult that it's almost impossible to solve the puzzle. But not quite. And some of us can see the clues better than others. So God sends out these spies to make sure we don't. Imagine that God's spies are certain dark personages, maybe he uses demons for this sort of work, I don't know. And these creatures watch. And listen. And they pay special attention to those of us who have a special gift for recognizing these patterns in the fabric of things. They watch us, and if we get close enough to the truth, they come to get us.

And I also think—at least I strongly suspect—that they don't just listen. I think they meddle. I think they like to play with us. If they can see that we love something too much, they make sure it gets taken away from us. Or they make sure people can't get together, so there's no comfort.

It's like that old novel where a man shoves a note under a door, and it goes under a rug, so a girl doesn't see it, so she never knows he loves her, and he thinks she doesn't want him, so their lives are different from what they might have been, and they're both unhappy forever. And this is just the sort of thing that's happened to me over and over again in my life. Just when I'm about to find some sort of love, some sort of happiness, achieve some sort of peace, just when I'm about to convince myself that nobody is watching me, that nobody is listening to me, that these patterns I keep seeing are just random manifestations of my human weakness for seeing connections, then something happens. Something always happens. And I catch a glimpse of them. Lurking just behind the curtains. Just out the window. Just on the other side of the door. Just out the corner of my eye. And I have to run away. Don't tell me that's just random events, or that it's just bad luck. That's a pattern. I know a pattern when I see one.

What I suspect is—and you can call this bad science or whatever, I don't care—what I suspect is that we all carry around these force fields. And when we touch, these force fields, or whatever they are, interpenetrate. And when they interpenetrate, all this energy interacts very powerfully. As in love. And there's a kind of storm in the head. Love is like a big electrical storm in your head. There's lightning, and the lightning makes a pattern. But lightning can also kill you. So it's very dangerous for a person who has more energy than most, who has a slightly higher body temperature than most. Something can't let this happen. Something can't let us just be happy. Happiness is not part of the pattern. And every time I reach out for it, I start to hear them whispering in the static in my phone calls. I see the evidence of their presence everywhere. A chair that seems to have been left in the wrong place when I wake up in the morning. I know the signs. I can see the patterns. And when I do, I have to run away, before they get me.

So I'm leaving. Don't try to follow me. I'm going someplace to hide, where they can't get me. All you can do to save yourself is keep in constant motion. But more and more I'm beginning to be afraid there's nowhere left to hide. They always find you. They can smell the desperation on you. They're drawn to love like flies to some poor dead thing in the street.

If you're honest with yourself, you know it's true. You know they're listening. You know they're watching. I'm going now. I'd like to stay and love you but I can't. They're watching me. For all I know, you could be one of them. But if you're not, if you just look quick enough, you can catch a glimpse of them. Just out the corner of your eye.

(The light fades on her and goes out.)

Portal

CHARACTER

There is one character, **OLMSTED**, a distinguished looking old man.

TIME

The time is 1903.

SETTING

The place is a house on an island in Maine.

AUTHOR'S NOTE

Vaux is pronounced Vox.

(In the darkness, eerie hurdy gurdy music is heard. Then, the sound of an elephant trumpeting in the distance. **OLMSTED**, *a distinguished looking old man, appears out of the fog and speaks. Vaux rhymes with flocks.)*

OLMSTED.

They've murdered poor Vaux. They found him floating at Gravesend. He's walking along the pier, watching the sun go down. He stops to purchase a bag of peanuts from a sinister looking Italian with a hurdy gurdy and a monkey, then has a chat with the owner of the pier, giving him advice for improving the beach. Vaux never had an idea in his life that didn't pour immediately out his mouth. All while he's talking, he notices that the Italian is watching him. The monkey is watching him.

He had hoped to live three more years, so we could finish Central Park. A Greenhouse. An Elephant House. They are washing the elephants at sunset. A carriage ride terminating at the Drowning Park. We should have buried Grant with a stake through his heart. Mulberry bend is a habitation of demons. No. These are not my thoughts. The demons are somehow putting them in my head. Their intention is to break the concentration of decent men. Keep in mind always that you practice God's profession. God was the first landscape gardener. Even as a child I left messages for God by pissing in the snow. But what was I saying? Something about—oh, Vaux. Poor Vaux. They are clouding my mind.

Found him floating in Gravesend Bay three days later. Partially devoured. Those are pearls that were his eyes. Forgot his spectacles, they said, dizzy spell, perhaps, stepped off the pier. This is what they would have you believe. But I know better. He wasn't the first. They murdered poor Harry. Called it a burst appendix, but I'll be damned if it was. Eliot died suddenly of meningitis, they called it. Downing. All of them. One by one they are eliminating everyone in a position to have unearthed their dark secrets. I do not believe in conspiracies, except for this one. And now they have kidnapped me and taken me to an island off the coast of Maine. They fear I will tell the world their secret, so they spread rumors that I am mad.

All right. I know how that sounds. I've been to the theatre, and I know a little something about madness. My father kept a madhouse, and I myself have constructed a number of madhouses. And knowing full well that my greatest fear has always been to be trapped in such a place, these insidious bastards have lured me to this island and left me here. The best we can hope for now is simple imbecility, I heard them tell my wife. Simple imbecility! A genius such as I! Did you hear that? That buzzing sound? No?

Listen carefully. There isn't much time. In Central Park, designed by Calvin Vaux and myself, there is a labyrinth of footpaths, with twenty gates. But somehow, through some sort of bizarre telepathic suggestion, or through the dream of a past life, we have placed each gate at the exact location of the portal to another dimension. And this series of murders, made to look like natural events, of persons connected with the design and creation of Central Park is in fact an insidious and demonic effort to conceal the subterranean inter-dimensional labyrinth to which the portals of Central Park lead. Only a select number of persons know of this labyrinth. I myself seem to have operated in a kind of trance as I helped select the locations of the portals. But some who know of this are not in a trance. Some who know of this are willing to do anything to protect the labyrinth to which the portals lead. It would seem clear to me that these creatures are not bound by time and space. I know it sounds mad. Hear me out. Just, I beg you, hear me out.

You must understand that I do not imagine that there is actually a labyrinth of pathways in the bedrock under Manhattan. Well, there is, if you consider the subways and the sewers. But I am speaking of something else here. That bedrock is coexistent with the pathways of another dimension or dimensions which somehow intersect with our universe at this point, this node, as it were, in a vast series of labyrinths within labyrinths, which is accessed by these portals. And I am by no means the first to have discovered this. It is my believe that the Indians knew. And some of the Dutch knew, before the English ever got here. In the personal diary of Peter Stuyvestant, governor of New Amsterdam, there exists a disturbing passage about the disappearance of children in the area now known as Central Park. But it is my conviction that the multidimensional labyrinth that one may access through these portals is far older than that, and that in the close vicinity of each of these portals is some sort of hatch, some sort of entrance, which has always been there, if one only knows how to access it. For the labyrinth is impossibly old and impossibly vast. It is the gateway to inter-dimensional travel which confounds all current understanding of space and time.

How did I come to be aware of this monstrous set of circumstances? Often what one learns best is what one learns by accident. One can acquire unexpected knowledge from anything, from humiliation in love to stepping over pigs in the street. One gradually becomes aware, over time. There are little signs. Little indications. At first, they seem meaningless. At first, one doesn't see the connection. One has been conditioned not to see these connections. But then, after a while, the correspondences are impossible to ignore. All these deaths, curious, unnatural, premature deaths, all of persons in a position to have discovered the secret. And then, standing at the portal, being drawn mysteriously to the portal, and standing there, at four in the morning, and being half aware that one is feeling a kind of intense vibration in the earth beneath one, and that one could hear, or almost hear, a faint, eerie, buzzing sound. I dare not even imagine what makes that monstrous buzzing.

There are many terrible things buried under the earth. There are layers and layers. And it is always dangerous to dig, because when you dig, you could find anything. We have no idea what is directly beneath us. In the earth lies the residue of all murders, from the beginning of time. All suffering comes from the earth and goes into the earth. And these layers, seemingly real in themselves, are at one and the same time also symbolic or projected representations of another reality which only appears to manifest itself here and now in this place at this time but which in fact is a part of the much greater labyrinth of all times and all places. And certain locations are a kind of nexus of energies, of pain, of human hope and despair. Manhattan island is such a place, and Central Park is its heart, and within that nexus of energies lies a labyrinth. And within that labyrinth, God only knows what horrors lurk.

Because all our attempts to build, to create structure, to control, are doomed, ultimately. Everything tends ultimately towards disorder. And the lords of the labyrinth, whoever they are, understand this well. They must even, perhaps, in the darkest part of their hearts, take a kind of pleasure in this, in the ultimate dissolution of all things. They have made an alliance with death.

But I shall not. I shall fight them to my very last breath. Landscape architecture is an attempt to make a kind of truce with nature, with God, with whatever powers that be there are. But the lords of the dark subterranean labyrinth care nothing about this. They mock all our efforts to create, to love, to be happy. And they must be resisted at all costs. One must never give in to them. Never. Because—wait, did you hear that? Listen. That buzzing noise. I know I heard it.

I am convinced they live among us. These creatures. Whatever they are. In the guise of politicians, doctors, religious leaders. They live among us to protect the portals. And they will do anything to prevent us from penetrating therein. They prevent us from creating. They block our pathetic attempts to reach out for love. It is monstrous. But here is what is really terrifying: that those other worlds, inner worlds, should lurk beneath the surface, secretly controlling our lives.

As a landscape architect, I have spent my life shaping the surface. But all the while, lurking below, underneath the surface, beneath the rational, where light cannot penetrate, lie other worlds, darker worlds—it is the existence of dark, inner universe upon universe within our world, within ourselves, perhaps, that drives one to such despair. Because inside this world is another, and inside that world another. The ego, what I have come to imagine is myself, is in fact only a surface. Beneath that surface is the hell of other dimensions, hidden dimensions, world upon world we cannot consciously, rationally know, which nevertheless determine how we behave and what we do and what we feel, who we love, who we hate, what we fear—that most of what is real cannot be comprehended by a sane person. Most of what is us cannot, either.

So perhaps I am mad after all. How comforting to think so. Perhaps I am mad after all. Wait. Do you hear that sound? A door is opening somewhere. The portal to another dimension. Only what they call the mad are granted brief glimpses into these hideous truths. But at such cost. At such cost.

And yet, there stands the portal before me. Soon I hope to have the courage to walk through that door.

(The light fades on him and goes out.)

Listening

CHARACTER, SETTING, & TIME

There is one character, Yvette, an old woman, who speaks to us from a circle of light in the darkness. Late twentieth century.

*(**YVETTE** speaks to us from a circle of light in the darkness.)*

YVETTE.

When the German tanks rolled into town, and the Nazi officers took over the chateau as their command center, our employers fled, but at the request of the Resistance we two servants remained, moving into the ancient secret passages behind the walls. We had to be very quiet, of course. If the Germans had had any suspicion we were there, we'd have been dragged out, lined up against the wall and shot. Our job was to listen. We listened to what was said. One of my grandmothers was German, and I learned to speak and understand a bit of the language from her, especially from the stories she told me when I was a little girl, and Ernst was born in Germany, although he came here as a child, and his parents would beat him if he didn't speak French— so we two were left behind to listen. Then, when the Germans had gone to bed, Ernst would sneak out through the secret tunnel into the back garden and convey the information to the Resistance through a hole in the crumbling garden wall.

There were two small, secret rooms, side by side, just off the passages in the attic, where we slept, Ernst in one room, me in the other. I'd wedge a piece of wood under the door of my room at night, just to be safe. It wouldn't have stopped the Nazis, but it stopped Ernst, at least for the time being.

In addition to being incredibly dangerous, our life there behind the walls could also be very frustrating. I didn't understand German as well as Ernst, and sometimes I had to guess at what they were saying, especially when they were on the telephone, and I could only hear one side of the conversation. One night I swear I heard two of them talking for three hours about the mating habits of zebras. And I thought, why are these Nazis talking for three hours about zebras? Have I completely misunderstood them? The mind wants to fill in the blanks. We make things up, without realizing that's what we're doing. Reality is a story we tell ourselves, like love.

And it was very dark in those passageways. We were forced to try to remember everything because there wasn't enough light to write things down while we listened and we couldn't risk having a lamp in there, in case the light might creep through a crack in the walls and be noticed. And we had to move very slowly, very carefully.

Ernst said we were like rats in the walls. And there were rats, and I was terrified of them. Sometimes, when I was listening, the rats would scuttle over my feet, or nibble on my ankles. It was all I could do to keep from screaming, but I couldn't move, and I couldn't make a sound.

Also, now and then I would actually get turned around in that maze of passageways, and not be completely certain where I was. I don't know why they were put in. It was a very long time ago. Somebody had to hide because somebody wanted to kill him because of his religion or some such thing. And at night I would dream that I was wandering in those passages and something was chasing me, and I was lost, and it was getting closer and closer, and I couldn't make a sound.

But as terrifying as this life was, it was also rather exciting. We would usually listen separately, from behind the walls of different rooms in the castle, so we could overhear as many conversations as possible, but sometimes Ernst would sneak up behind me in the dark when I was listening, and put his hands on my buttocks. He knew I couldn't make a sound or risk any sort of commotion that might alert the Nazis on the other side of the wall, so he put his hands anyplace he wanted to. I would scold him afterwards, but what I was actually feeling at the time was a complex and remarkably intense mixture of fear, anger, and sexual arousal. Sometimes I wondered if the only reason Ernst stayed was so he could caress my breasts and buttocks in the dark while I listened.

I put up with it, because Ernst was not just doing the brave thing I was doing, he was also sneaking into the back garden at night under the noses of the German guards, risking his life to get the information to the Resistance. I supposed that at some point I would probably allow him to make love to me.

But after a while, I began to have doubts. Some of his interpretations of what the Nazis were saying seemed wrong to me. I never dared to challenge him, because I was so uncertain of the language myself, but I began to ask myself, Did Ernst really understand German as much as he seemed to? Could he have been exaggerating his knowledge to impress me? Was he making up half the things he said he heard? And even more disturbing, was he really able to sneak out into the back garden at night to give the Resistance the information, or did he perhaps just hang out in the tunnel for a while and then come back to our hiding place in the morning?

Anything seemed possible. Our world was a shadow world. We were people who lived in shadows. Our life was like a dream. We overheard reality, muffled, spoken in a language of which we had an imperfect understanding. When Ernst was gone and the Germans were asleep, I'd sneak into the pantry through a little secret door behind the shelves and steal a bit of food, just enough for us to survive, but not enough to arouse suspicions. And that was our life, for many months, during the war.

Then one night Ernst didn't come back. I waited and waited. I was physically ill with worry. I went down into the tunnel and peeked out into the back garden, but nobody was there. Had he crawled over the garden wall and escaped? I was tormented and miserably lonely. And I was trapped in those secret passages all by myself with the rats, and I couldn't make a sound. Many terrible thoughts ran through my head. What if they had captured him, and were torturing him? What if they got him to tell them about the secret passages, and about the listening, and about me? They might be coming to kill me at any moment. It was enough to drive a person completely out of her mind.

But I forced myself to remain calm. I didn't know what else to do, so I just kept listening, and then, when they'd all gone to bed, I'd sit in my little secret room and write down as much as I could remember in a little notebook by moonlight. I had a window. My great fear was that one day one of the Germans would be walking in the garden, and happen to look up, and realize that there was a window for which he could find no corresponding room.

This went on for weeks. I found myself unable to sleep, and would lie awake at night, staring into the darkness, listening to the rats scuttling in the passageways. Then I'd be sleepy all day, and it would make me careless and clumsy. And one morning, when I could barely stay awake, I must have dropped off, because I found myself naked in bed with Ernst, and he was making love to me while the Germans laughed and made crude comments from behind the walls, and the next thing I knew, my head was hitting the inside of the study wall with a loud clunk, and I woke up, and realized that the conversation between the German officers on the other side of the wall had abruptly stopped.

I stood very still, but I was shaking so hard I could barely stand up. I heard the floor boards creak as the Germans moved towards the wall. They were speaking to each other in hushed tones, examining the wall. They were very close to me, just on the other side of the wall. One of the Germans said something to the other one. I couldn't quite catch it, but I was pretty sure I heard the word 'ax.' He was telling the other German to go and get him an ax. I was certain then that I was going to die, and I wanted to run away down the passageways, but I couldn't move. He was so close to me, just on the other side of the wall. He could probably hear me breathing, or even my heart pounding. It was a weirdly intimate moment.

Then the other one came back with the ax. I closed my eyes and began to pray. There was some more whispering from their side. They were trying to decide the best place to smash through the wall. Then the telephone rang.

The phone was answered. A rapid fire conversation followed, most of which I didn't catch. But it was clear that something was wrong. Then I heard the sound of gunfire, and suddenly there was an enormous explosion that shook the house. Then another. And just like that, the Germans had forgotten all about the mysterious noise on the other side of the wall. I heard them running out of the room, and the sound of agitated voices shouting all over the house. I ran down the passageways and huddled in the tunnel to the garden. The sounds of explosions and gunfire continued long into the night. Eventually I fell asleep.

When I woke up, I could hear birds singing in the garden. I made my way back through the passageways into the house. The house was silent. It was empty. The Germans had gone. My first instinct was to run out into the street, but I knew that wasn't a good idea. They might still be in the town. There might be snipers. In their haste, they'd left plenty of food. I decided the best thing to do was to stay in the house until I was certain it was safe to come out. I didn't want anybody to know I was there, so I only moved about in the house itself in the night, in the dark. The rest of the time I spent in the passageways, where I felt safer.

A few days later the house was taken over by American soldiers. My English wasn't good, so it was not clear to me what they were saying most of the time, but I felt as if, had I just walked out from behind the walls they might have thought I was a spy and shot me. Or that they would have turned me out into the street, and, having no family and no place to go, I'd end up living in the street, and starve to death. Here, at least, I had a safe place to sleep, and a full pantry to steal from.

Later, the Americans moved on, and new people moved into the house. They were not the same family as before. It must have been sold, or inherited, I didn't know. But by now it was the only home I'd ever really known. So I just stayed.

I don't know how many years I've been here now, living behind the walls. They're really a very interesting family. They quarrel and gossip and fight, and at night I can hear them making love. I've grown very fond of them. The wife insists that food keeps disappearing from the pantry, but the husband tells her she's imagining it. The daughter thinks there's a ghost. And actually, that's what I feel like. If there are ghosts, this is probably what they do. Observe us quietly, invisibly, for their own entertainment, a kind of living theatre.

I've grown comfortable here. Although it's very lonely. Often, when I hear them making love at night in the creaky old bed upstairs, I think about Ernst touching me in the darkness. Yes. I think this is what ghosts do. They lurk in the darkness, listening.

(The light fades on her and goes out.)

Nothingness

I am first affrighted and confounded with that forlorn solitude in which I am placed in my philosophy, and fancy myself some strange uncouth monster, who not being able to mingle and unite in society, has been expelled all human commerce, and left utterly abandoned and disconsolate.
– David Hume, *A Treatise Of Human Nature*

*Now canst thou comprehend
the measure of the love
which warms me toward thee
when I forget our nothingness
and treat shades as a solid thing.*

– Dante, *Purgatorio, Canto XXI.*

If it be nothing, I shall not need spectacles.

– William Shakespeare, *King Lear*

CHARACTER & SETTING

There is one character, **BEN**, a man of 62, who speaks to us from a circle of light surrounded by darkness.

*(**BEN**, a man of 62, from a circle of light on an otherwise dark stage.)*

BEN.

There's a story about the great Scottish philosopher David Hume, undoubtedly an exaggeration, but I like this version of it: Hume is sitting alone in his study one night, working out his proof that there is no necessary relationship between what we usually consider to be a cause and the subsequent event that we are accustomed to thinking of as an effect, or that what we call reality is anything more than a set of appearances. And the further he delves into the implications of these ideas, the more he begins to feel an uneasiness that develops into deep, irrational panic, and suddenly he finds himself doubting the reality of anything, including himself, and feeling, to his horror, a growing conviction that if he opened the door to his study and looked out, nothing would be there.

Hume is terrified. He knows it's foolish, but he can't stop shaking. Somehow, with a tremendous act of will, he forces himself to go to the door, hesitates for a moment, and then opens it. He sees the familiar hallway, hears the ticking of the clock to his right, and down the hall to the left, the reassuring click of billiard balls. He walks down the hall, touching the walls to make sure they feel solid, opens the door to the billiard room, and finds his friends there playing. It's comforting to him, the way the billiard balls respond to the stroke of the pool cue, roll across the table, and hit other balls, which move in trajectories determined by the direction and force of the ball that strikes them. If cause and effect is an illusion, then it's an apparently consistent illusion, and choosing to live within the framework of that apparent consistency, illusion or not, is what allows one to remain sane. So, despite the fact that there is no real assurance that the billiard balls are always going to behave the way one expects them to, and no proof that the future will be consistent with what we think we have observed in the past, Hume is reassured. After a while he excuses himself and walks back down the hall, past his study, past the ticking clock to his bedroom. He opens the door and steps into oblivion, falling helplessly head over heels into absolute nothingness.

It's a dream, of course. He wakes up suddenly, nearly tumbling off the chair in his study where he's been dozing. He puts his palms firmly on the desk, breathing heavily, while the rapid beating of his heart slows. Of course there is cause and effect. His desk feels perfectly solid under his hands. In any case, an illusion which is a consistent illusion is indistinguishable from reality. But what exactly do we mean when we speak of reality? What we call reality is not a characteristic of an external universe, but simply a product of the capabilities and limitations of our own minds to comprehend that bombardment of sensations which appears to us to be an external universe. If our capacity to understand increases, reality changes, because reality can only mean "reality for us." We can never experience directly an objective reality because to experience is by definition subjective. This is not to assert that there is no external reality, but only that if there is, we can't know it as reality, because all that we have to know it with are our perceptions, and our perceptions are limited by our capacity to perceive. And my understanding of those perceptions is limited by the capacity of my reason, which is larger than my cat's but not as large as Einstein's, just as his would not be as large as that of a person of double his intelligence. The ability of a creature with double the intelligence of Einstein to comprehend reality would be to Einstein as Einstein's ability to comprehend reality would be to that of my cat.

This is the sort of thing I sit and think about, living alone here by the woods. When you live with other people it's easier to construct a hypothetical concept of an external world, because even though you're all experiencing subjectively, the sum of those subjectivities works as a kind of rough stand-in for an objective reality. But when you live alone, you don't have that. Everything is like a dream. You begin to get slowly cut off from other people's sense of reality, and from your sense of the reality of other people. This is why saints and mystics have traditionally gone off to the wilderness, so they can be alone with their own subjective impressions, unpolluted by the jabbering static of other people.

But that doesn't work, because the more isolated you become, the more people there are jabbering inside your head. And the people in your head become just as real to you as the people you think are outside your head. The play of our lives, now farce, now melodrama, always ultimately tragedy, is cast entirely with the inhabitants of our brains. Love is the people in your head.

I keep thinking about my father's pool table. When I was fourteen, my father and I were left permanently alone together, and I was angry and sullen and in despair, and really quite impossible to reach. My father tried various ways to help me out of this morass of anger and depression I lived in, but nothing was working. Then one day an enormous package arrived. I thought it must be a mistake. We had almost no money, and I couldn't imagine what on earth he would have ordered that would be so big. We managed to get it down the steps into the basement somehow and took the cardboard off and I saw that it was a pool table. We had almost no money and my father had sent for a pool table. It was very unlike him to do anything that impulsive. I wondered for a moment if he wasn't losing his grip.

I helped him set it up, angry at being taken away from my reading, which was the only real pleasure I took in the world at that time. But my father had a bad leg from the war, and needed my help, so I did it. It was rather handsome—not green, but a kind of golden tan color. Two pool cues and a set of balls. I wanted to go upstairs, but my father insisted that I stay and play a game with him. And this was the beginning of my instruction on how to play pool.

I was really terrible at it at first. My father had spent a good part of his youth at the local pool hall, and was in all things involving hand eye coordination much better than me in any case, so he won every game. And my frustration only fueled my anger, and I kept whacking the balls so hard they would fly off the table.

You're shooting too hard, said my father. You've just got to give it the right amount of force to put it where you want it to go. He taught me how to put English on the ball, how to use the banks, how to play Eight Ball and Nine Ball and another game that he and I seem to have invented together. I was very angry and very bad at it. He was very calm and very good at it. He never let me win. He just showed me how to accomplish what I wanted. All that anger was getting me nowhere. If I wanted something, I had to learn to calm down and focus, clear my mind of everything else, just pay attention to the task at hand. If you hit the ball on a certain spot, with a certain force, no more or less than you needed, you could knock the other ball into the pocket. And gradually I got better, and got interested in the game as its own reality, and now and then I would beat him. He would pretend to be annoyed at this, but I don't think he was, really. He was teaching me something else. It wasn't about pool at all. I was so stupid I really didn't understand this until many years later. A lot of the things my father taught me were like this. He'd take me one place to show me something else. And he never would explain.

My father's been gone five years now. I moved home to take care of him when he got sick and lost his leg. And I helped him learn to walk again. And eventually he could make it down the basement steps again so we could play pool.

The table is old now. A big rip is taped up. The banks are dead. The cloth is torn. The pool cues are crooked, and the balls have chips in them. And the table is grotesquely warped. You can't really play a serious game of pool on it any more, although sometimes I still do just shoot, by myself. Most of the time the table is covered, and the cats sleep on it. They like it very much. Time remains impossibly strange to me. I live alone in my father's house.

To get old, especially to get old in relative isolation, is to live more and more deeply inside the theatre in your head. Hope gives way to regret. Desire is grudgingly replaced by resignation. The body becomes a stranger as one moves closer and closer to opening the door that leads back into the nothingness from which one has entered the play.

So David Hume's heart has stopped pounding. He feels better now. Then he looks across the room at the door. In order to get to his bed, he must walk across the room and open that door, with absolutely no assurance that there's anything whatsoever beyond it. Of course, he does get up, and he does walk over to that door, as he's done thousands of times in the past, and he opens the door, and everything is there, just as he imagined it would be. But he also knows, as I know, that one night he will open that door and before he knows what's happening step into absolute nothingness.

(The light fades on him and goes out.)

Muse

For Anna Contessa

CHARACTER & SETTING

There is one character, **JASMINE**, a woman of 28, who speaks to us from a circle of light on an otherwise bare stage.

(**JASMINE**, *a woman of 28, speaks to us from a circle of light on an otherwise bare stage.*)

JASMINE.
    Just because I'm in your head—
    I mean, I know I'm in your head.
    But of course it doesn't last.
    Because it's necessary to—
    because a person needs to—
    If I was there always, you'd
    just keep wanting more.
    Things I couldn't give.
    It's not that I want to go away.
    I don't want to go away.
    It's just that—

    Sometimes, walking in the city at night,
    I've felt as if somebody was following me.
    And then turned around.
    And it was nobody.
    That's how I knew it was you.

    If I stayed, you'd get tired of me.
    Sometimes people get tired.
    I'm kind of a handful.
    I'm exhausting.
    Like trying to keep
    cats in a bucket.
    And after a while,
    they just can't deal with it.

    It's not that I don't trust you.
    It's that you don't trust me.
    And one of us is wrong.

Because the darkness in you,
which is something only I can see,
there are shapes in the darkness,
people I used to know.
Time is all jumbled in there.

You don't know me.
And I don't know you.
And maybe it's better that way.
Because love is—
Love is—
I don't know what love is.
I don't know anything about that.

I know you think I should
get out of this place, and
come and live with you
and the raccoons forever,
because you hate this place,
you think this is not a good place,
but there are lovely things
even in Hell.

And maybe people here
do bad things to me
but you mustn't blame them
because sometimes your friends
are the people who kill you.

No, I don't mean that.
I don't know why I said that.
Things just bubble up
out of me.

I don't know where that came from.
I don't know where anything comes from.

If I'm your muse,
then who's mine?

Why don't I get a muse?
I don't want to be my own muse.
That's the definition of crazy.
Well, one of many.
And I should know.
I'm the whole encyclopedia.
Not the encyclopedia of crazy.
The whole encyclopedia
and everything in it.
Isn't that what you said?
I'm the girl in your head.

I always have been.
I'm the Anima Mundi.
I'm the last tarot card.
I'm the naked girl who is the World.
That's what you told me.

Well, that's a lot of pressure, you know?
When you love a person too much
it puts a lot of pressure on them.
It's not fair to put that sort
of pressure on a person.

But that's not why I need to go.
The reason I need to go,
the reason I need to go is,
this is not love because—
well, all right, maybe it is love, but—
okay, so it's love, but that doesn't mean,
that doesn't mean—okay,
I don't know what it means.

It's always a mistake to
try and understand.

That's a form of control,
from your dark side.

And to control your muse
is to kill her.
Which is why she gets scared
and runs away.

You pretend to be worried about me.
Well, all right, you're worried about me.
But there's no reason to be.
Well, okay, there's some reason to be.
Maybe a lot of reason to be.

But that's not your job.
Your job is just to write,
to keep on writing while you can.
Although I'm not sure how
you're going to do it,
when I'm not here,
but that's the beauty of it,
because even when I'm gone,
I'm here in your head,
just as even when I'm here,
I'm gone.

That doesn't make any sense.
But then, some of the best things
I ever said don't make any sense.

But it doesn't really matter.
Because in the middle of the night,
lying alone in the middle of the night—
listening to the ticking of the clocks,
lying alone in the middle of the night,
trust me, you're going to find—
you're going to find that,
after a little time has passed—

    (Pause.)

All right. I'll stay a while.

But just for a little while.

I'm not unpacking all my clothes
or anything,
because everything is—
everything is—
I don't know what everything is.

Maybe I could be your muse
and you could be mine.

Okay?

Okay.
I'm going to kiss you now.
Or I would.
But you're not here.

>*(The light fades on her and goes out.)*

www.ingramcontent.com/pod-product-compliance
Lightning Source LLC
Chambersburg PA
CBHW071841290426
44109CB00017B/1891